THE REVOLUTIONARY WAR LIBRARY

African Americans and American Indians Fighting in the Revolutionary War

JOHN MICKLOS, JR.

Enslow Elementary

an imprint of

 Enslow Publishers, Inc.
40 Industrial Road
Box 398
Berkeley Heights, NJ 07922
USA

http://www.enslow.com

Frontispiece: During the American Revolution, people had to decide which side they were on. Crispus Attucks (left) was an African American slain during the Boston Massacre in 1770. Mohawk Chief Joseph Brant (right) was a key British ally.

Enslow Elementary, an imprint of Enslow Publishers, Inc.

Enslow Elementary® is a registered trademark of Enslow Publishers, Inc.

Library of Congress Cataloging-in-Publication Data

Micklos, John.
  African Americans and American Indians fighting in the Revolutionary
War / written by John Micklos, Jr.
    p. cm. — (Revolutionary War library)
  Summary: "Learn about the contributions of African Americans and
American Indians to both sides during the Revolutionary War"—Provided
by publisher.
  Includes bibliographical references and index.
  ISBN 978-0-7660-3018-3
  1. United States—History—Revolution, 1775-1783—Participation,
African American—Juvenile literature. 2. United States—History—Revolution,
1775-1783—Participation, Indian—Juvenile literature. I. Title.
  E269.N3M53 2008
  973.3'08—dc22
                        2007048509

ISBN-10: 0-7660-3018-0

Printed in the United States of America.

10 9 8 7 6 5 4 3 2 1

To our readers: We have done our best to make sure all Internet Addresses in this book were active and appropriate when we went to press. However, the author and the publisher have no control over and assume no liability for the material available on those Internet sites or on other Web sites they may link to. Any comments or suggestions can be sent by email to comments@enslow.com or to the address on the back cover.

Every effort has been made to locate all copyright holders of material used in this book. If any errors or omissions have occurred, corrections will be made in future editions of this book.

♻ Enslow Publishers, Inc., is committed to printing our books on recycled paper. The paper in every book contains 10% to 30% post-consumer waste (PCW). The cover board on the outside of each book contains 100% PCW. Our goal is to do our part to help young people and the environment too!

Illustration credits: *Washington Crossing the Delaware River, 25th December 1776.* 1851 (oil on canvas) (copy of an original painted in 1848). Leutze, Emanuel Gottlieb (1816-68) / Metropolitan Museum of Art, New York, USA / The Bridgeman Art Library, 21; Colonial National Historical Park, 10, 11; The Granger Collection, New York, 5, 6, 8, 15, 16, 22, 26, 30, 33, 34; Independence National Historical Park, 1 (right), 28; © iStockphoto.com/Dan Tobin, 4; © 2008 Jupiterimages Corporation, 36, 40 (top right); Courtesy of the Prints and Photographs Division, Library of Congress, 1 (left), 7, 13, 14, 27, 40 (bottom left), 41 (top left); National Archives, 18, 35; New Hampshire Historical Society, 41 (bottom left); © North Wind/North Wind Picture Archives, 12; © OTTN Publishing, 38; Used under license from Shutterstock, Inc., 19, 32, 41 (bottom right); From the Collection of the State of South Carolina, 20; Woolaroc Museum, Bartlesville, Oklahoma, 39.

Cover Photos: Courtesy Deborah Johnson (background soldiers, used throughout book); Courtesy of the Prints and Photographs Division, Library of Congress (left); Independence National Historical Park (right), © iStockphoto.com/Duncan Walker (flag in background).

Produced by OTTN Publishing, Stockton, N.J.

Table of Contents

CHAPTER ONE

On the Eve
of the Revolution

Their bayonets gleamed in the early morning sun. On April 19, 1775, British soldiers marched into the town of Lexington, Massachusetts. There they faced off against a colonial militia company.

Soon shots rang out. The fighting continued later in nearby Concord. The first shot that day became known as "the shot heard 'round the world." These battles marked the start of the Revolutionary War.

Like many of his friends, Peter Salem fired his musket at the British that day. Unlike most of the others, Salem was a slave. He had signed up for the militia because his master had promised him freedom if he did so.[1]

In 1775, 2.5 million people lived in the 13 colonies. Of this total, about one in five—or 500,000 people—were slaves.[2] Most of these slaves lived in the southern colonies. A much smaller number lived in the North.[3]

In 1619, about twenty black people had been brought

Peter Salem was a slave who fought with the Americans. After the Battle of Concord, he saw action at the battles of Bunker Hill, Saratoga, and Stony Point.

This painting shows English colonists at Jamestown examining the first slaves brought to North America in 1619.

TO BE SOLD, on board the Ship *Bance-Island*, on tuesday the 6th of *May* next, at *Aſhley-Ferry*; a choice cargo of about 250 fine healthy NEGROES, juſt arrived from the Windward & Rice Coaſt. —The utmoſt care has already been taken, and ſhall be continued, to keep them free from the leaſt danger of being infected with the SMALL-POX, no boat having been on board, and all other communication with people from *Charles-Town* prevented.

Auſtin, Laurens, & Appleby.

N. B. Full one Half of the above Negroes have had the SMALL-POX in their own Country.

(Left) An advertisement for a slave auction in South Carolina. Slaves could be found in every American colony, but most slaves lived in the South: Georgia, South Carolina, North Carolina, Virginia, and Maryland.

(Bottom) Iron shackles were fastened to the ankles of slaves to prevent escape.

aboard a ship to the British colony of Jamestown in Virginia. Scholars believe these men, who were probably seized as slaves in south-western Africa, were among the first blacks in America.

Over the following decades, thousands of black Africans were brought into the colonies as slaves. The long

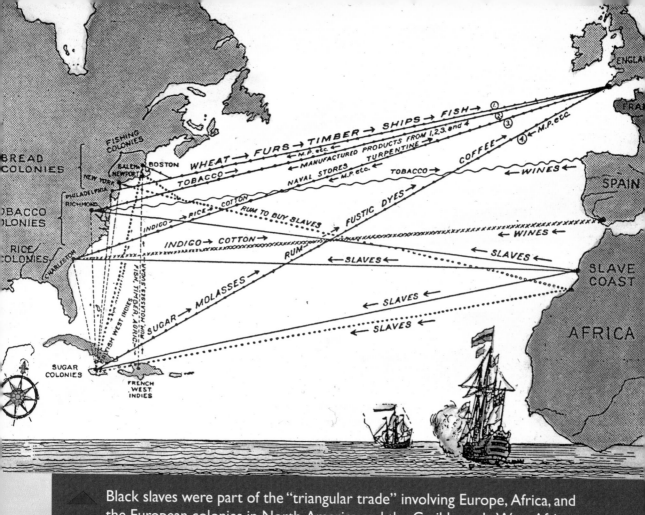

FISHING COLONIES
BREAD COLONIES
TOBACCO COLONIES
RICE COLONIES
SALEM BOSTON NEWPORT NEW YORK PHILADELPHIA RICHMOND CHARLESTON

WHEAT → FURS → TIMBER → SHIPS → FISH → ④
MANUFACTURED PRODUCTS FROM 1,2,3, and 4
M.P. etc.
TOBACCO →
NAVAL STORES TURPENTINE →
M.P. etc.
RICE → COTTON
RUM TO BUY SLAVES
INDIGO → COTTON →
RUM →
INDIGO → RICE → COTTON
FUSTIC DYES →
← SLAVES
SUGAR → MOLASSES →
← SLAVES
SUGAR COLONIES
FRENCH WEST INDIES
FISH TIMBER AGRIC.
LYONS EXECUTION MFG.

TOBACCO →
COFFEE →
② ③
④ M.P. etc.
← WINES ←
← WINES ←
← SLAVES ←
← SLAVES ←

ENGLA
FRA
SPAIN
SLAVE COAST
AFRICA

Black slaves were part of the "triangular trade" involving Europe, Africa, and the European colonies in North America and the Caribbean. In West Africa, European merchants provided goods such as guns and alcohol to African traders in exchange for slaves. The slaves were then transported across the Atlantic and sold in the Caribbean or North America for products such as cotton, tobacco, sugar, molasses, and rum (all of which slave labor helped produce). These products were then shipped back to Europe.

voyage across the Atlantic Ocean from Africa was brutal. Many slaves died during the trip.

Once in America, slaves lived a hard life. Most worked in the fields all day. They grew crops such as rice and

8

tobacco. Slaves working in the Deep South tended to have harsher and shorter lives than slaves further north.[4]

Most African Americans in the northern colonies did not live as slaves. A few in the South were free as well. They were able to hold jobs. They could own houses. Still, they did not enjoy the same rights as white people. Whites did not view them as equals.

Many whites also did not view Indians as equals. At the start of the Revolutionary War, there were about 200,000 American Indians living east of the Mississippi River.[5] They came from 85 separate Indian nations.

★ ★

UNEQUAL TREATMENT

The Declaration of Independence stated that "all men are created equal."[6] In many cases, however, blacks were not treated as equals. Many of the Founding Fathers owned slaves. Even among the colonists who did not own slaves, most believed that black people were not as good as white people.

Many colonists did not think highly of American Indians, either. The Declaration of Independence called them "merciless Indian Savages."[7]

Most wanted to stay out of the conflict. They simply wanted to live in peace.

Still, the American Indians knew the war affected them. Many tribes fought with settlers who had moved onto their lands. These tribes wished to keep their lands. They wanted to preserve their way of life. With this in mind, most

From the start, Indians had a complicated relationship with European colonists. The Indians wanted to trade for goods such as metal tools and firearms. But they did not want colonists settling on their lands.

This painting shows American Indians ambushing two colonists caught outside their settlement. As greater numbers of settlers moved onto Indian lands, fighting became more common.

tribes sided with the British. They thought the British would help protect them from the land-hungry settlers.

As the war began, most blacks in America were slaves. Even those who were free lacked the rights that whites had. They hoped the war might somehow help them gain more rights. Meanwhile, American Indians feared losing their land and their way of life. They hoped the war might somehow help them preserve both.

CHAPTER TWO

Which Side to Choose?

When the Revolutionary War began in 1775, colonists fought to protect their rights as English subjects. Most remained loyal to the king. By the next year, the focus had turned to liberty.

The Declaration of Independence said it all. America wanted freedom from England. Nearly 500,000 slaves throughout the colonies wondered if the war might bring them freedom as well.

Few slaves found freedom before the war. Some were set free by their masters. A few managed to earn enough money to pay for their freedom. Many tried to escape. While some succeeded, most failed. Those who were captured faced harsh punishment.

Some slaves knew of a slave case that had been settled in England in 1772. In that case, a slave named James Sommersett had been purchased in Virginia. He was taken to England, where he escaped. He was later recaptured. The judge ruled that Sommersett could not be returned to his master against his will.[1]

AN
ARGUMENT
IN THE CASE OF
JAMES SOMMERSETT
A NEGRO,
LATELY DETERMINED BY
THE COURT OF KING's BENCH:
Wherein it is attempted to demonstrate
THE PRESENT UNLAWFULNESS
OF
DOMESTIC SLAVERY IN ENGLAND.
TO WHICH IS PREFIXED
A STATE OF THE CASE.

By Mr. HARGRAVE,
One of the COUNSEL for the NEGRO.

LONDON:
Printed for the AUTHOR:
And sold by W. OTRIDGE, opposite the New
Church, in the Strand.
M. DCC. LXXII.

In James Sommersett's 1772 case, a judge ruled that slavery was illegal in England. Slavery was still permitted in the American colonies, however.

THE FIRST MARTYR

Tensions ran high in Boston, Massachusetts, in early 1770. British troops occupied the city. That made the residents angry. On the evening of March 5, the anger led to violence. A crowd of patriots gathered around the British soldiers on duty.

Crispus Attucks

The mob yelled insults and threw snowballs. The British soldiers raised their guns in defense. The crowd dared them to fire. Then a club flew through the air. It hit one of the soldiers. Soon shots rang out. Three men near the front of the mob fell dead. Eight others were wounded. Two of them later died. The incident became known as the Boston Massacre.

One of the first to die was Crispus Attucks. Attucks was part black and part American Indian. Attucks and the others who died were called martyrs. These are people who die to support a cause.

A Boston newspaper reports on the funerals of Crispus Attucks and others killed in the Boston Massacre.

Other slaves reasoned that if they could get to England, they too could be free.

Slave owners always feared that their slaves would rise against them. It was not an idle fear. In South Carolina, for instance, there were far more slaves than non-slaves.[2] Slave rebellions did happen from time to time. In April 1775, just as the war began in New England, three slaves in Virginia were convicted of trying to lead rebellions.[3]

Slave owners across the South feared that the British would provide weapons to help slaves rebel. In the spring of 1775, the Earl of Dunmore, Virginia's royal governor, increased those fears. He revealed a plan "to arm all my own Negroes and receive all others that will come to me whom I shall declare free."[4] A few months later, he declared all slaves free if they would join the British and "bear arms" in the war.[5]

On November 7, 1775, Lord Dunmore offered freedom to any black slaves who fought against the rebellious colonists in Virginia.

Soon many slaves were trying to escape to the British side. Some ended up on British ships off the coast of Virginia. Many died there of disease. In Georgia, the British housed 200 escaped slaves on an island near Savannah. In March 1776, colonists attacked the island. They were aided by some local American Indians. They slaughtered many of the former slaves.[6]

Slaves faced hard decisions. When the British army came near, many fled to join it. Others did not. What if life

A French soldier painted this picture of American troops, including a black infantryman (left), at the siege of Yorktown in 1781.

★ ★

WASHINGTON'S PLEA

American leaders tried hard to win the backing of the American Indians. At the very least, they wanted to keep them from siding with the British. "Brothers: I am a Warrior," General George Washington said to the Delaware Indians. "My words are few and plain; but I will make good what I say. 'Tis my business to destroy all the Enemies of these States and to protect their friends."[7] Washington tried to make it sound as though the British were weak. He tried to convince the Delaware tribe to back the colonists.

with the British proved to be no better? What if the British lost? Then the slaves would be returned to their angry masters. There were no easy choices.

In the end, thousands of slaves did flee to the British. They still led a hard life. The British often put them to work as blacksmiths, carpenters, or road builders. Sometimes the former slaves were paid for their work. Often they were not. Some were even sent as slaves to islands in the West Indies.[8]

Some African Americans joined the patriot cause. Many of these men were free blacks from the northern colonies. Others were slaves seeking freedom. Many of these slaves did receive their freedom in return for serving in the army.

American Indians found themselves facing the same types of choices. For years, some tribes had done well by trading with the colonists. Others fought with settlers who tried to take their land. Some tribes had learned to play the American colonists and the British against each other. By threatening to support one side or the other, they attempted to make both sides treat them well.

The war made things tougher. Whichever side won would have great power. American Indians wanted to support the side they thought would treat them most fairly. Most tribes

An American soldier speaks with American Indian leaders, trying to convince them to support the colonists in their war against Great Britain.

TRIBAL ALLIANCES

Catawba—backed the colonists

Cherokees—mostly backed the British

Chickasaws—backed the British

Delaware—backed the colonists

Iroquois—mostly backed the British

Seminoles—backed the British

believed that side was the British. But they also did not want to back the losing side. Then they would lose, too. Tribal leaders made choices based on what they thought would be best for their people.

The war split some tribes. For instance, some Cherokees sided with the British. Others wanted to stay neutral.

In the end, most American Indians sided with the British. The British promised to keep settlers out of their lands. The Indians hoped a British victory would protect their way of life.[9]

CHAPTER THREE

African Americans in the Army

Sleet and snow pelted the Continental soldiers on Christmas night in 1776. General George Washington led his small army across the ice-choked Delaware River in boats. He hoped to launch a

This famous painting shows General Washington crossing the Delaware River in 1776 to attack Trenton. Prince Whipple, a slave who helped the Continental Army, is pictured rowing in the front of Washington's boat.

surprise attack on the British outpost in Trenton, New Jersey. Helping row Washington's boat was a slave named Prince Whipple. With Whipple's help, Washington got across the river safely. His troops surprised the enemy and won the battle. This triumph helped turn the tide of the war.[1]

A few months earlier, young fifer John Greenwood had seen a black soldier wounded in the back of the neck at the Battle of Bunker Hill. Blood ran down the man's back.

This drawing of the Battle of Bunker Hill may show a slave named Asaba Grosvenor reloading his musket. Asaba was the servant of an American officer named Thomas Grosvenor.

Greenwood asked if the soldier was all right. The man said he was going to get the wound treated. Then he planned to return to the battle. Greenwood said he had been afraid. After seeing that man's bravery, he no longer felt scared.[2]

At first, General Washington did not want black soldiers in the Continental Army. When he took command, Washington issued an order saying that neither "Negroes, boys unable to bear arms, nor old men" were to be enlisted.[3] He feared that white soldiers from the South would refuse to serve with black soldiers. Some southerners feared that giving guns to blacks could lead to a slave uprising.

By the end of 1775, many of the Continental Army volunteers had gone home. The army was shrinking. Washington asked the Continental Congress to decide whether black people could serve. Congress said blacks who were already in the army could reenlist. Many did. Indeed, many black soldiers served for long periods.

★ ★

NAMES OF FREEDOM

Many slaves did not have last names. Others were given the last name of their master. Free blacks often took new names. The last names of black soldiers in the Continental Army often showed why they were fighting. One regiment had black soldiers named Jeffrey Liberty, Pomp Liberty, Sharp Liberty, and one with the last name of "Freedom."[4]

SUCCESSFUL SPY

James Armistead, a slave, watched as British general Charles Cornwallis moved his army to Yorktown, Virginia. Armistead was a trusted servant to Cornwallis. He pretended to spy for the British. Meanwhile, he was really spying for the Americans. Armistead informed the Marquis de Lafayette of the British army's movements. He provided many important details. In turn, General Lafayette—a French volunteer who served with the Continental Army—passed the news on to General Washington.

Washington thought he could trap the British troops at Yorktown. He rushed his soldiers south from New York. They were joined by a French fleet. They surrounded Cornwallis and forced him to surrender. That defeat caused the British to give up the war effort.[5]

A total of about 200,000 men served in the Continental Army or a militia unit during the course of the war.[6] Black soldiers made up only a small part of this number. In all, about 5,000 blacks served. Hundreds of these men were slaves. Many were set free in return for their service.[7]

Others, such as Salem Poor, were freemen. Poor served from 1775 through the end of the war. He suffered through the hard winter at Valley Forge. So did many other black soldiers. In fact, at one point blacks made up almost 10 percent of Washington's army.[8]

On the other side, many slaves found freedom with the British forces. Some joined units called Black Pioneers. Some former slaves formed their own units. An escaped slave known as Colonel Tye led one such group. He fought in many skirmishes across New Jersey.[9]

In 1775, Lord Dunmore of Virginia invited slaves to join the British. Eight hundred or more slaves did so. Dunmore formed the men into a regiment. In the end, however, he did not lead them into battle. Many died from smallpox. The following summer, Dunmore sent those who remained off to join other British forces.[10]

Many blacks served as sailors. Life aboard the ships was hard. Still, it was better than being a slave. Many colonies had their own navies. In Virginia's navy, at least four African Americans served as pilots. One led an attack on a British ship.[11]

CHAPTER FOUR

American Indians in the War

Smoke rose from burned houses. Crops lay ruined. The summer of 1778 brought war to the Mohawk Valley of New York. First, British and Iroquois Indians defeated the patriot soldiers in the area. Then they attacked American settlers. They burned houses and barns. In return, patriot patrols burned Indian villages and crops.

The fighting was brutal. Each side accused the other of killing innocent women and children. Most of the claims were false. A few were true. Reports of the fighting caused hatred for the Iroquois among the settlers.[1]

Most American Indians did not want to be drawn into the war between the colonists and the British. Still, the outcome mattered a great deal to them. Many tribes faced the threat of land-hungry settlers.[2]

Jane McCrea was a young woman who lived in New York. Her family were loyalists, which meant that they supported the British. However, in 1777 she was kidnapped and murdered by members of an American Indian tribe allied with the British army. This brutal act, depicted in this nineteenth-century illustration, turned many loyalists against the British.

MOHAWK LEADER

Joseph Brant was a Mohawk leader. As a youth, he had the chance to go to school. There he learned to speak and write English. For a while, he worked for the British. He helped them in their relations with the Indians. He also helped translate parts of the Bible into the Mohawk language.

Joseph Brant

When the Revolutionary War started, the six tribes of the Iroquois met. The Mohawks were one of these tribes. At first the tribes voted to stay neutral. Brant later convinced four of the six tribes to support the British. The other two backed the colonists.

During the war, Brant served as head war chief for his tribes. He also was named a captain in the British army. After the war, England gave him a huge tract of land along the Grand River in Canada. He brought nearly 2,000 Mohawks to live there. The town of Brantford is named after him.[3]

With this in mind, most American Indians favored the British. Still, many tribes tried to stay out of the fighting as best they could. In many cases, they could not. War raged all around them. They ended up getting pulled into it.

Most American Indians who fought sided with the British. A few fought for the Continental Army.

Leaders in the Continental Congress tried hard to keep the American Indians neutral. They knew how dangerous it would be if large numbers of tribes went to war against them. Virginia governor Patrick Henry pleaded with the colonists to treat the Indians well. "Any Injury done them," he said, "is done to us while they are faithfull."[4]

Still, that was easier said than done. In the lightly settled areas of the north and west, there was

★ ★

BROKEN PROMISE

In 1778, the United States and the Delaware tribe signed a treaty. It contained a remarkable clause. The Delaware agreed to let the American army pass through their lands. They agreed to feed and guide the soldiers. In return, the treaty gave the Delaware tribe the right to have a representative in Congress. In effect, this would have created a new state. Delaware chief White Eyes was pleased with the treaty. There was just one problem. The treaty needed the approval of Congress. Congress did not agree to the plan.[5]

With a small army, George Rogers Clark captured a large area of frontier territory from the Indians and British.

frequent fighting between American Indians and settlers. Many of the battles were vicious. Settlers often destroyed entire Indian villages and farms. Indians burned cabins and mills.[6]

On the western frontier, the British and their Indian allies held the upper hand at first. Then American George Rogers Clark began a daring campaign. He had only 200 men. Still, he conquered an area twice the size of Great Britain. His small force captured British forts across a wide area. He helped America stake its claim to a huge tract, or area, of land. When the war ended, Britain ceded (gave up) this land to the United States.[7]

To the south, the Cherokee tribe was split apart. The older chiefs wanted peace with the colonists. The young warriors wanted war. They hoped to slow down the spread of white settlers onto their lands. The warriors launched many raids against settlers. Then a force of 6,000 soldiers from four colonies marched out to take revenge. The soldiers were told to "cut up every Indian corn-field, and burn every Indian town."[8]

Within a few months, the Cherokees were beaten. In May 1777, they signed two treaties with four colonies. As a result of these treaties, the Cherokees ceded rights to more than 5 million acres of land. This was an area as big as the state of New Jersey.[9]

For the most part, American Indians suffered as a result of the Revolutionary War. Many tribes were drawn into the conflict. Others still faced white settlers moving into their lands. After the war, things got even worse for most of the tribes. Settlers streamed west. There was no turning back the tide.

CHAPTER FIVE

Aftermath

The Revolutionary War brought independence to the United States. It did not bring such benefits to African Americans or American Indians. Slavery continued for 80 more years. In fact, the number of slaves rose from fewer than 500,000 in 1770 to almost 700,000 in 1790.[1]

Some people thought slavery was wrong. Still, most whites continued to view blacks as inferior. Also, slaves were needed to support the economy. Plantation owners in the South especially needed slaves to work on their huge farms.[2]

One by one, northern states passed laws banning slavery. There were few slaves there. Slave labor was not needed to run the economy. But even in the north, most whites did not treat blacks as equals.[3]

A few years after the Revolution ended, Congress enacted the Northwest Ordinance.

Cotton, tobacco, rice, and sugar were among the most important crops produced in the southern states. However, to make money growing these crops, planters needed a lot of workers. Southern farmers relied on black slaves to do the difficult work of planting and harvesting.

This law outlined how new territories and states would be formed from the western lands won as a result of the war. Slavery was outlawed in these lands. But the U.S. Constitution, which was passed in 1789, protected slavery. It said that the slave trade could not be banned before 1808.[4]

★ ★ ★ ★ ★ ★ ★ ★ ★ ★ ★ ★ ★ ★ ★ ★ ★ ★ ★

WASHINGTON AND SLAVERY

George Washington had mixed feelings about using blacks in the army. He knew they could be good soldiers. He had a black aide named Billy Lee. Lee served him throughout the war. Washington then gave him his freedom. Still, Washington did not view blacks as equals. He owned more than 100 slaves.[5]

George Washington speaks with a foreman while his slaves harvest hay on his plantation at Mount Vernon.

Washington did treat his slaves well. Over time, his feelings about slavery changed. In his will, he freed all his slaves.[6]

An ORDINANCE for the GOVERNMENT of the TERRITORY of the UNITED STATES, North-West of the RIVER OHIO.

BE IT ORDAINED by the United States in Congreſs aſſembled, That the ſaid territory, for the purpoſes of temporary government, be one diſtrict; ſubject, however, to be divided into two diſtricts, as future circumſtances may, in the opinion of Congreſs, make it expedient.

Be it ordained by the authority aforeſaid, That the eſtates both of reſident and non-reſident proprietors in the ſaid territory, dying inteſtate, ſhall deſcend to, and be diſtributed among their children, and the deſcendants of a deceaſed child in equal parts; the deſcendants of a deceaſed child or grand-child, to take the ſhare of their deceaſed parent in equal parts among them: And where there ſhall be no children or deſcendants, then in equal parts to the next of kin, in equal degree; and among collaterals, the children of a deceaſed brother or ſiſter of the inteſtate, ſhall have in equal parts among them their deceaſed parents ſhare; and there ſhall in no caſe be a diſtinction between kindred of the whole and half blood; ſaving in all caſes to the widow of the inteſtate, her third part of the real eſtate for life, and one third part of the perſonal eſtate; and this law relative to deſcents and dower, ſhall remain in full force until altered by the legiſlature of the diſtrict. ————— And until the governor and judges ſhall adopt laws as herein after mentioned, eſtates in the ſaid territory may be deviſed or bequeathed by wills in writing, ſigned and ſealed by him or her, in whom the eſtate may be, (being of full age) and atteſted by three witneſſes; — and real eſtates may be conveyed by leaſe and releaſe, or bargain and ſale, ſigned, ſealed, and delivered by the perſon being of full age, in whom the eſtate may be, and atteſted by two witneſſes, provided ſuch wills be duly proved, and ſuch conveyances be acknowledged, or the execution thereof duly proved, and be recorded within one year after proper magiſtrates, courts, and regiſters ſhall be appointed for that purpoſe; and perſonal property may be transferred by delivery, ſaving, however, to the French and Canadian inhabitants, and other ſettlers of the Kaskaskies, Saint Vincent's, and the neighbouring villages, who have heretofore profeſſed themſelves citizens of Virginia, their laws and cuſtoms now in force among them, relative to the deſcent and conveyance of property.

Be it ordained by the authority aforeſaid, That there ſhall be appointed from time to time, by Congreſs, a governor, whoſe commiſſion ſhall continue in force for the term of three years, unleſs ſooner revoked by Congreſs; he ſhall reſide in the diſtrict, and have a freehold eſtate therein, in one thouſand acres of land, while in the exerciſe of his office.

There ſhall be appointed from time to time, by Congreſs, a ſecretary, whoſe commiſſion ſhall continue in force for four years, unleſs ſooner revoked, he ſhall reſide in the diſtrict, and have a freehold eſtate therein, in five hundred acres of land, while in the exerciſe of his office; it ſhall be his duty to keep and preſerve the acts and laws paſſed by the legiſlature, and the public records of the diſtrict, and the proceedings of the governor in his executive department; and tranſmit authentic copies of ſuch acts and proceedings, every ſix months, to the ſecretary of Congreſs: There ſhall alſo be appointed a court to conſiſt of three judges, any two of whom to form a court, who ſhall have a common law juriſdiction, and reſide in the diſtrict, and have each therein a freehold eſtate in five hundred acres of land, while in the exerciſe of their offices; and their commiſſions ſhall continue in force during good behaviour.

The governor and judges, or a majority of them, ſhall adopt and publiſh in the diſtrict, ſuch laws of the original ſtates, criminal and civil, as may be neceſſary, and beſt ſuited to the circumſtances of the diſtrict, and report them to

The Northwest Ordinance, passed by Congress in 1787, outlawed slavery in the Northwest Territory. Eventually, five new American states—Ohio, Indiana, Illinois, Michigan, and Wisconsin—would be formed from the Northwest Territory.

In 1808, Congress did ban the importation of slaves.

This meant new slaves could not be brought into the country.

The law did not, however, free the slaves who were already in

the United States. Slavery remained a problem for decades.

35

After January 1, 1808, it became illegal to ship new slaves into the United States. However, slaves who were already in the country, along with their descendants, could still be bought and sold. This drawing shows a slave sale in South Carolina, around 1850.

In the end, the issue helped lead to the Civil War. The North's victory in that war finally brought slavery to an end.

For Indians, the Revolutionary War led to loss. Many lost their lives in fighting. Then, after the war, more and more settlers moved west. As a result, many American Indians lost their lands and homes. Most tribes had supported the British. When the British lost, they lost, too.

The Treaty of Paris—the treaty between the United States and England to end the Revolutionary War—did not mention Indians at all. Some British leaders were outraged.

★

ABOLISHING SLAVERY

The 13th Amendment to the U.S. Constitution ended slavery. "Neither slavery nor involuntary servitude . . . shall exist within the United States," it declared. The 13th Amendment was passed by Congress on January 31, 1865. It was ratified, or formally approved, by the states on December 6, 1865.[7]

They had made treaties with the American Indians. They had tried to preserve Indian land. They thought those treaties should be honored.

The Americans disagreed. They had won the war. They believed that allowed them to keep the land the British had controlled. The Treaty of Paris set the boundaries of the United States. Those boundaries extended from Canada in the north to what is now the northern border of Florida in the south, and from the Mississippi River in the west to the Atlantic Ocean in the east. This included many lands that belonged to various Indian tribes. The Americans told the Indians that they had chosen the wrong side in the war.

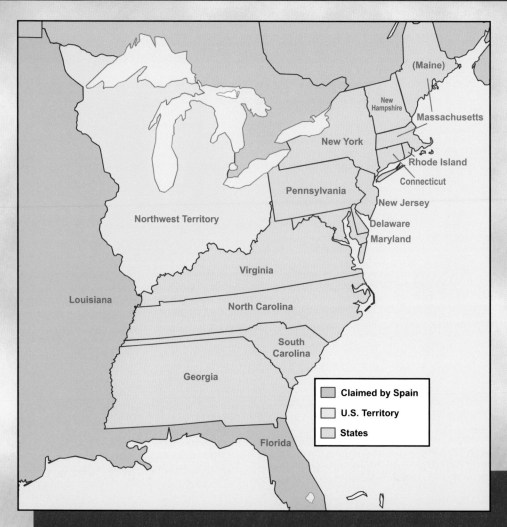

The United States after passage of the Northwest Ordinance, 1787.

The American Indians could not rely on anyone to protect their rights. They were treated as a conquered people.[8]

Congress tried to be fair. In 1787, the Northwest Ordinance set rules about how the western land should be

As Americans pushed into the western territories, Indians were forced to leave their lands. This painting shows Cherokee Indians moving to a new territory in what today is Oklahoma.

settled. It said that the Indians should be treated with "good faith." It promised that "their lands and property shall never be taken from them without their consent."[9]

This promise proved empty. Settlers kept pressing westward. Congress could not stop them. Treaties did not stop them. Many tribes fought to save their lands. In some cases, they were able to hold on for a little while. In the end, however, nothing could stop the westward push. For the Indians, the triumph of the American Revolution proved to be the start of a great tragedy.

In all, the American Revolution had brought important changes to many different groups of people. Only time would tell the full impact of those changes.

REVOLUTIONARY WAR TITLE
REVOLUTIONARY WAR
TIMELINE

George Washington

In 1763, King George III prohibits settlers from moving west of the Appalachian Mountains. This is supposed to prevent conflict between American colonists and Indians.

In April, the Revolutionary War begins with fighting at Lexington and Concord, Massachusetts. During the course of the war, some 5,000 African Americans will fight for the patriot cause. Many black slaves will join the British army.

In January, Congress approves George Washington's decision to let free blacks reenlist in the Continental Army.

In May, the Cherokee tribe signs a pair of peace treaties with four American states. In those treaties, the defeated Cherokees cede 5 million acres of land.

In early summer, a British force that includes hundreds of Indian warriors lays siege to Fort Stanwix, an American post in New York's Mohawk Valley.

Prewar	1775	1776	1777

During the Boston Massacre of March 5, 1770, Crispus Attucks is shot and killed by British soldiers.

The Boston Massacre

In 1772, a British judge rules that James Sommersett, a slave who escaped while in England, cannot be forced to return to his Virginia master.

At the Battle of Bunker Hill on June 17, a slave named Peter Salem is believed to have shot Major John Pitcairn as the British officer rallied his men to overrun the American position. Salem's action is credited with saving many Americans.

In November, Virginia's royal governor promises freedom to slaves who agree to fight against the rebellious Americans.

In July, colonial leaders approve the Declaration of Independence. It criticizes King George III for encouraging slave uprisings and attacks against colonists by American Indians, who are referred to as "merciless Indian savages."

A 6,000-man American force defeats Cherokee warriors in the South.

At the beginning of August, an 800-man American militia, including about 40 Oneida Indians, is sent to relieve the defenders of Fort Stanwix. On August 6, a force of 1,200 Mohawk Indians and British soldiers ambushes the American militia at Oriskany Creek. The battle sparks a war between the Oneida and Mohawk tribes.

Washington rallies the troops at the Battle of Monmouth.

More than 700 black Continental soldiers fight alongside their white comrades in the Battle of Monmouth Court House in New Jersey.

American generals John Sullivan and James Clinton lead a campaign against the four Iroquois tribes that have allied themselves with the British.

In 1781, slave James Armistead, a patriot spying for the Continental Army, reports that a large British army has moved to Yorktown, Virginia. George Washington decides to try to trap the British there. He marches thousands of Continental soldiers from New York to Virginia.

Congress passes the Northwest Ordinance. It sets up a process for turning new territories in the area into states. Slavery is prohibited in the new lands, and Congress promises to treat American Indians with "good faith."

1778   1779   1781–1783   1787

Mohawk chief Joseph Brant (Thayendanegea), an ally of the British, leads Iroquois warriors in a series of raids against American settlers in northern New York.

On August 29, 1779, General Sullivan defeats about 1,000 Iroquois warriors in a large battle at Newtown, near present-day Elmira, New York. After the battle, the Americans burn dozens of Indian villages and destroy their crops. Many Indians die of starvation and disease during the following winter.

British forces at Yorktown surrender on October 19, 1781. This is the war's last major battle.

The Treaty of Paris, which officially ends the war, is signed on September 3, 1783. The treaty cedes to the United States a vast expanse of land between the Appalachian Mountains and the Mississippi River.

In September, representatives of the states sign the final draft of the United States Constitution. The document permits the importation of slaves until at least 1808.

John Sullivan

The U.S. Constitution

CHAPTER 1: ON THE EVE OF THE REVOLUTION

1. Gary B. Nash, *The Unknown American Revolution: The Unruly Birth of Democracy and the Struggle to Create America* (New York: Viking, 2005), p. 225.

2. Gordon S. Wood, *The American Revolution* (New York: Modern Library/Random House, 2002), p. 56.

3. Ray Raphael, *A People's History of the American Revolution: How Common People Shaped the Fight for Independence* (New York: The New Press, 2001), p. 246.

4. Dale Taylor, *The Writer's Guide to Everyday Life in Colonial America From 1607–1783* (Cincinnati, OH: Writer's Digest Books, 1997), pp. 65–66.

5. Nash, p. 247.

6. Declaration of Independence, from U.S. History.org Web site, <http://www.ushistory.org/declaration/> (October 16, 2007).

7. Ibid.

CHAPTER 2: WHICH SIDE TO CHOOSE?

1. "Black Presence, Rights: Slave or Free," Web site of the National Archives (United Kingdom), <http://www.nationalarchives.gov.uk/pathways/blackhistory/rights/slave_free.htm> (October 15, 2007).

2. Dale Taylor, *The Writer's Guide to Everyday Life in Colonial America From 1607–1783* (Cincinnati, OH: Writer's Digest Books, 1997), p. 69.

3. Ray Raphael, *A People's History of the American Revolution: How Common People Shaped the Fight for Independence* (New York: The New Press, 2001), p. 245.

4. Gary B. Nash, *The Unknown Revolution: The Unruly Birth of Democracy and the Struggle to Create America* (New York: Viking, 2005), p. 160.

5. Alfred W. Blumrosen and Ruth G. Blumrosen, *Slave Nation: How Slavery United the Colonies & Sparked the American Revolution* (Naperville, IL: Sourcebooks, Inc., 2005), p. 122.

6. Raphael, p. 261.

7. "Speech to the Delaware Chiefs." From "George Washington: A Collection." The Online Library of Liberty, <http://oll.libertyfund.org/?option=com_staticxt&staticfile=show.php%3Ftitle=848&chapter=101782&layout=html&Itemid=27> (October 15, 2007).

8. Raphael, pp. 263–264.

9. John M. Thompson, *The Revolutionary War* (Washington, DC: National Geographic Society, 2004), p. 114.

CHAPTER 3: AFRICAN AMERICANS IN THE ARMY

1. Gary B. Nash, *The Unknown American Revolution: The Unruly Birth of Democracy and the Struggle to Create America* (New York: Viking, 2005), p. 225.

2. Bruce Chadwick, *The First American Army: The Untold Story of George Washington and the Men Behind America's First Fight for Freedom* (Naperville, IL: Sourcebooks, Inc., 2007), p. 8.

3. Thomas Fleming, *Liberty! The American Revolution* (New York Viking, 1997), p. 151.

4. Ibid.

5. Madison Gray, "James Armistead: Patriot Spy." *Time* magazine Web site, Black History Month: Unsung Heroes. <http://www.time.com/time/2007/blackhistmth/bios/01.html> (February 15, 2008).

6. Fleming, *Liberty!*, p. 334.

7. Joseph C. Morton, *The American Revolution* (Westport, CT: Greenwood Press, 2003), p. 79.

8. Thomas Fleming, *Washington's Secret War: The Hidden History of Valley Forge* (New York: Smithsonian Books, 2005), pp. 142–143.

9. David Hackett Fischer, *Washington's Crossing* (New York: Oxford University Press, 2004), pp. 169–170.

10. Nash, pp. 162–163.

11. Ray Raphael, *A People's History of the American Revolution: How Common People Shaped the Fight for Independence* (New York: The New Press, 2001), p. 291.

CHAPTER 4: AMERICAN INDIANS IN THE WAR

1. Gary B. Nash, *The Unknown American Revolution: The Unruly Birth of Democracy and the Struggle to Create America* (New York: Viking, 2005), p. 257.

2. Robert Middlekauff, *The Glorious Cause: The American Revolution, 1763–1789* (New York: Oxford University Press, 2005), p. 574.

3. George L. Marshall, Jr., "Chief Joseph Brant: Mohawk, Loyalist, and Freemason," Archiving Early America Web site, <http://www.earlyamerica.com/review/1998/brant.html> (October 22, 2007).

4. Ray Raphael, *A People's History of the American Revolution: How Common People Shaped the Fight for Independence* (New York: The New Press, 2001), p. 213.

5. Ibid., pp. 215–216.

6. John M. Thompson, *The Revolutionary War* (Washington, DC: National Geographic Society, 2004), p. 114.

7. Ibid., pp. 116–117.

8. Raphael, p. 224.

9. Ibid., pp. 226–227.

CHAPTER 5: AFTERMATH

1. Ray Raphael, *A People's History of the American Revolution: How Common People Shaped the Fight for Independence* (New York: The New Press, 2001), p. 296.

2. Robert Middlekauff, *The Glorious Cause: The American Revolution, 1763–1789* (New York: Oxford University Press, 2005), p. 571.

3. Ibid., p. 572.

4. "The Constitution and Slavery," Constitutional Rights Foundation Web site, <http://www.crf-usa.org/lessons/slavery_const.htm> (May 11, 2008).

5. David McCullough, *1776* (New York: Simon & Schuster, 2005), p. 47.

6. Forrest McDonald, "Today's Indispensable Man," in Gary L. Gregg II and Matthew Spalding, eds., *Patriot Sage: George Washington and the American Political Tradition* (Wilmington, DE: ISI Books, 1999), p. 28.

7. "Primary Documents in American History: 13th Amendment to the U.S. Constitution," Library of Congress Web site, <http://www.loc.gov/rr/program/bib/ourdocs/13thamendment.html> (October 22, 2007).

8. Wilcomb E. Washburn, "Indians and the American Revolution," American Revolution.org Web site. <http://americanrevolution.org/ind1.html.> (October 22, 2007)

9. "Text of the Northwest Ordinance," Archiving Early America Web site, <http://www.earlyamerica.com/earlyamerica/milestones/ordinance/text.html> (October 22, 2007).

CHAPTER NOTES

benefit—Something good or helpful; a payment, gift, or other advantage.

brutal—Savage, cruel, or harsh.

cede—To give up; to yield or surrender.

clause—A distinct portion of a formal document, will, or treaty.

convicted—Found guilty of a crime.

enacted—Put into action.

inferior—Lower in place or position; seen as less good.

involuntary—Against one's wishes.

martyr—Someone who dies or suffers to support a cause.

militia—A military unit made up of citizens who are not full-time soldiers but agree to serve in an emergency.

neutral—Not taking sides, especially in an argument or war.

patriot—An American who supported independence from Great Britain during the Revolutionary War period.

preserve—To keep.

prohibited—Not allowed.

ratified—Formally approved by a governing body, such as Congress.

rebellion—Armed resistance to a government or ruler; resistance to authority.

residents—People who live in a certain place.

servitude—Forced labor or slavery.

skirmishes—Fights between small groups (as opposed to full battles).

tract—An area or piece of land.

uprising—A violent revolt against persons or groups who hold power.

BOOKS

Brennan, Linda Crotta. *The Black Regiment of the American Revolution*. North Kingstown, RI: Moon Mountain Pub., 2004.

Cohen, Stephanie. *Joseph Brant: Iroquois Leader in the Revolution*. Boston: Houghton Mifflin, 2004.

Harper, Judith E. *African Americans and the Revolutionary War*. Mankato, MN: Child's World, 2000.

Keller, Kristin Thoennes. *The Slave Trade in Early America*. Mankato, MN: Capstone Press, 2003.

INTERNET ADDRESSES

American Indians and the American Revolution by Collin G. Calloway

http://www.americanrevolution.com/AmericanIndiansintheRevolution.htm

Kid Info page on the American Revolution

http://www.kidinfo.com/American_History/American_Revolution.html

PBS series *Africans in America*, Part 2: "The Revolutionary War, 1750–1805"

http://www.pbs.org/wgbh/aia/part2/2narr4.html

FURTHER READING

INDEX

Numbers in ***bold italics*** refer to captions.